£14.75

Thomson, Ruth
 Elena in Cyprus.
 1. Cyprus–Social life and customs–
 Juvenile literature
 I. Title   II. Thomson, Neil
 956.45′04   DS54.9
 ISBN 0–7136–2922–3

A & C Black (Publishers) Limited
35 Bedford Row, London WC1R 4JH

© 1987 A & C Black (Publishers) Limited

Acknowledgements

The map is by Tony Garrett

All rights reserved. No part of this publication may be reproduced, stored in a retrieval system, or transmitted in any form or by any means, electronic, mechanical, photocopying, recording or otherwise, without the prior permission in writing of A & C Black (Publishers) Limited.

Filmset by August Filmsetting, Haydock, St Helens
Printed in Hong Kong by Dai Nippon Printing Co. Ltd

Elena in Cyprus

Ruth and Neil Thomson

A & C Black · London

Hello. My name is Elena and I'm ten and a half. Here I am in the park with the rest of my family. My brother is called Antonis. He's four years younger than me.

Our family is Greek Cypriot and we live in Limassol, a busy seaside town and port on the south coast of Cyprus. In the southern part of the island everyone speaks Greek, but in the north they all speak Turkish.

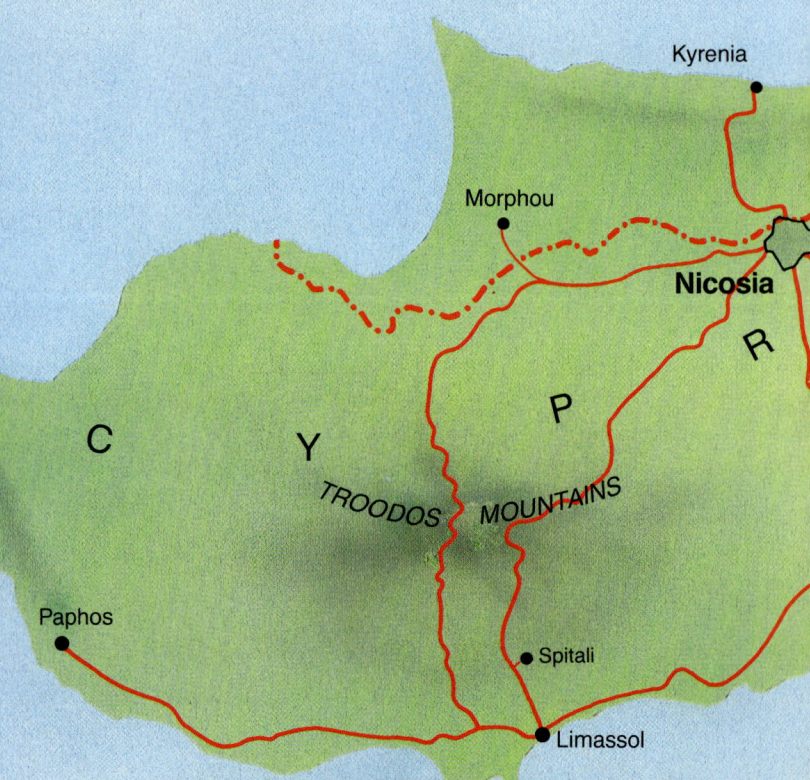

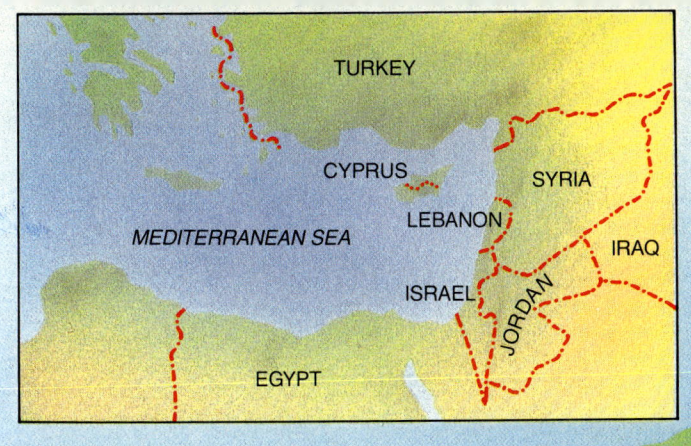

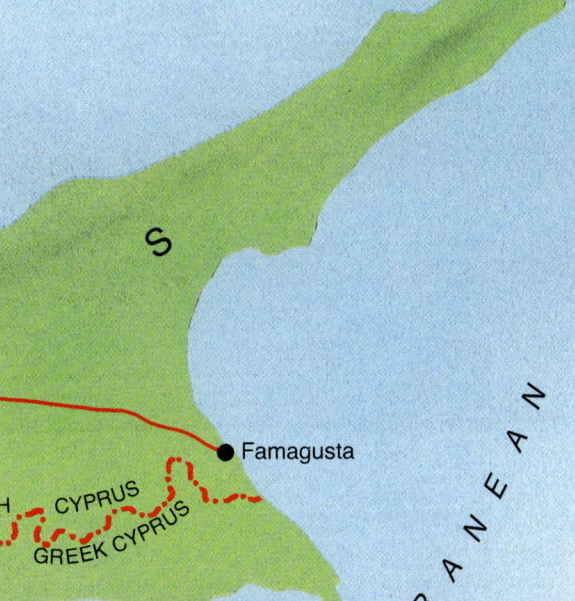

My dad, Georghiou, has lived in Limassol all his life. My mum, Anna, was born in a village near Paphos, but came to Limassol when she was fourteen, to go to school.

Most of the buildings along the sea front are hotels and apartment blocks for tourists. They have nearly all been built in the last five years and more are going up all the time.

We live near the centre of the old town, where the streets are narrow and winding. Dad's always complaining about the traffic. The yellow sign with the red arrow, half-way down the road, points to the quiet side road where we live.

Our house belongs to my mother. My grandparents arranged the marriage between Mum and Dad, and had the house built for Mum before she was married. Dad says that when Antonis and I are grown up, he will divide the house into two flats and give one to each of us. Then Mum and Dad will move into a small flat by themselves.

The house is modern and has two floors. Downstairs, there is a kitchen and a sitting room. Upstairs, there are three bedrooms and the bathroom. I share a room with Antonis. It's very small so Mum makes us keep it tidy.

This is the roof of the house. The solar panels are for heating our water. Cyprus is sunny all year round and Mum says just two hours of sunshine a day are enough to heat all the water we need.

The main market is quite near our house. It's right next to the central bus station. Every day, people from villages around Limassol come in by bus with the fresh food they've grown. They set up their stalls in the square, next to the indoor market. Dad goes there every couple of days to buy all our fruit and vegetables.

Once a week the whole family goes to a big supermarket to buy groceries. Dad told me that when I was little, there weren't any supermarkets at all in Limassol.

Mum still prefers the small local shops where she can buy fresh bread, milk and eggs. Often when she's forgotten something, she sends me to the shop round the corner.

In the new part of Limassol, there are expensive clothes shops and hamburger and pizza restaurants. We never go into any of them. Dad says they are just for tourists.

Dad is an environmental health inspector. One of his jobs is to make sure that the sea doesn't get polluted by waste from the big hotels on the sea front. Limassol has no main sewage system, so dirty water is collected in underground tanks and chemicals are added to make it safe. Then it is pumped into a large pit and left to soak slowly into the ground.

Dad checks the plans of all new hotels to make sure that the pits will be big enough for all the waste and far enough from the sea not to cause pollution. Here's Dad visiting one of the hotels to take a sample of its cleaned waste water. He will send the sample to a laboratory to check whether the water has been properly cleaned.

In the afternoons, after work, Dad is always busy. He has a studio down the road from our house, where he goes to paint. Every so often, he holds an exhibition. He's also got a small boat, which he is repairing for the summer. Soon I'll be old enough to go fishing with him, though he says there aren't many fish around Limassol any more.

Antonis and I both go to the same school, which is just down the road from our house. School starts at half past seven. It only takes us five minutes to get there, so we don't have to get up too early. Lots of children come by school bus from the outskirts of Limassol.

We go to school every day except Sunday. On Saturdays, we start with an assembly in the playground. One of the children always writes a prayer for assembly and reads it over a loudspeaker so the whole school can hear. Then we listen to the Greek national anthem and a group of children bring forward the Greek and Cypriot flags, which are raised on the flagpole.

There are thirty children in my class. The girls sit in pairs in the middle of the class. The boys sit in a semi-circle around the outside. I always sit with my friend Maria. There are five Marias in my class! Sometimes it's very confusing for the teachers.

We have lessons in Greek, mathematics, geography, religion, science, art and music. We learn both Greek and Cypriot history. Twice a week, we have PE in the playground. That's me in the middle. I haven't knocked a hurdle over yet, even though I'm not very tall.

One of my favourite subjects is music. The teacher plays a tape on a cassette recorder and we all sing along. She conducts and we play our instruments. We learn songs from Greece and Cyprus. At the moment, we are learning a traditional song to sing on Greek National Day.

This year, everyone started learning an instrument. Half the class chose the mandolin and the rest chose recorders. I chose the mandolin. My dad bought me one of my own so that I could practise at home.

On Greek National Day, everyone has the day off. Each school in Limassol sends a group in their uniform to parade down the main street. The parade celebrates the time when Greece freed itself from Turkish rule. I hope my class will join in next year.

The whole town turns out to watch. The streets get so crowded that it's hard to see anything at all. Luckily, since I'm small, people usually let me wriggle my way through to the front, so I get a good view.

Today in geography, we are learning about a town called Morphou, in Northern Cyprus. The teacher has asked me to come up to the front to tell the class what I have read about it. None of my class has been to Morphou although my teacher once went a long time ago. We can't visit it now because it's out of bounds for Greek Cypriots.

Two years before I was born, in 1974, the Turkish army took over the northern part of Cyprus. All the Greek speaking people who lived there had to leave their homes and their land and come to the southern part of the island. The Turkish people in the south had to move north. Since then, people from one part of Cyprus aren't allowed to visit the other.

Many of the refugees from the north came to Limassol. Some of the children came to study at my school. They drew these pictures to show everyone in their class what they had seen and what had happened to them.

They drew the battles between the Greek and Turkish armies and the bombing of buildings. They also drew pictures to show what it was like to live in a refugee camp.

My teacher has kept the pictures from that time to remind us and help us learn about what has happened to our island. She says they are very precious.

School finishes at half past twelve. When I come home, I feed our bird and if its cage is dirty, I clean it out. A friend of ours caught the bird and gave it to us as a present. We keep it in the yard. Mum hopes it will bring us luck.

Then I try to do my homework straightaway, so that I'll have the afternoon free. Sometimes I help Mum with the house, and lay the table for lunch.

We eat our main meal at two o'clock, when Dad comes home from work. Often we start with a soup, called avgolemono. Mum makes it with chicken broth, eggs, rice and lemon juice. For main course, we have chicken, fish or meat with potatoes and vegetables or salad. There's fruit to finish. I like bananas and melon best.

Sometimes, Mum makes a batch of little cakes. My favourites are called ladies' fingers. They are thin little packets of pastry stuffed with crushed nuts and honey. Grown-ups like them with coffee, but I have home-made lemonade with mine.

Two afternoons a week, we go to see my grandparents. They live in a new house not very far from us. My grandfather built the house to give to my Aunt Rea, who lives there as well. When Aunt Rea gets married (which my grandmother hopes will be soon), my grandparents will move to a small flat on their own.

My grandfather used to be a carpenter for the British Forces, who have a base at Akrotiri, a few kilometres outside Limassol. Now he has retired, he has plenty of time to play with us and make us toys. He also spends a lot of time in the local café, talking politics with his friends.

Grandmother always gives us a few pence to spend, so Antonis and I either go and buy sweets or rush out to the ice-cream van when it comes past at five o'clock. Then, while all the grown-ups chat outside on the terrace, Grandmother lets us watch cartoons on the television. She brings us snacks of bread and honey, or haloumi (goat's cheese) – delicious!

Early on Sunday mornings, Mum and I go to church. We are Greek Orthodox Christians. The church we go to is called St Michael's. I like the inside of the church. The walls and ceiling are decorated with patterns, mosaics and pictures showing events in Christ's life.

This Sunday after the service, a woman shares round some little cakes. Mum says I must keep some back for Antonis. On our way back home, we always go past the mosque, which has been locked for as long as I can remember. This is the place where the Turkish Cypriots used to pray when they lived on this part of the island.

Most Turkish Cypriots are Moslems, but since the time when they had to leave for the north of Cyprus, no one has used the mosque. Mum says that before I was born, when the mosque was in use, people used to be called to prayer five times a day over the loudspeakers. Now they are silent.

On Sundays, my Uncle Demos sometimes invites us for lunch in the country. He has some land near Spitali. The rest of the family come along too if they can. It's about forty minutes away in the car and there's plenty to see on the way.

The road outside Limassol climbs and winds its way into the hills. Now it's springtime, the trees are in blossom and all along the side of the road, there are masses of poppies, daisies and other wild flowers. There is plenty of new grass for the sheep and goats. I expect the goatherds are glad they don't have to walk a long way to find pasture for their animals.

Uncle Demos works in Limassol, but spends his spare time on his plot of land.

He has planted lemon, grapefruit, orange and olive trees, so we always know where to go for our fruit.

He used to keep sheep and sell their milk and meat. But last year he had to sell them, because he didn't have time to look after them properly. Now he only keeps chickens. My cousins and I like feeding them when we get a chance.

Dad and Uncle Demos get busy preparing lunch. It's my favourite – barbecued lamb, or souvla. Dad threads chunks of lamb on to enormous skewers, which are turned over hot coals. From time to time, he rakes the coals so the meat will cook evenly.

In the meantime, Mum and my aunts make salads. Aunt Polimnou wraps some potatoes and fish in silver foil and puts them in hot ashes to bake.

While we're waiting, my cousins and I play chase or skipping games. Marianna is always messing around when she's in the middle – she's also much better at skipping than I am!

At last it's time for the picnic. There's always plenty of food, because nobody quite knows how many people are going to turn up for lunch. Uncle Demos just says 'Come to lunch one Sunday – I'm always here then'. He hopes that one of these days everyone will turn up on the same Sunday – that'd be really good fun.